Flower on Still Water at Dawn

A Collection of Poems

By Carl Weaver

Copyright ©2026 by Carl Weaver
All Rights Reserved
ISBN: 978-1-944616-49-6
Published by Broken Column Press
BrokenColumnPress.com

Lighting lantern

Lighting lantern
flash of sorrow
a moment of clarity
as rain pummels the panes
of my window and draws in
the cool nighttime air

Lost in a world of our own

Your eyes are like crystal in my heart
solid and clear, warm but distant
When we touch, our skin is no longer a barrier
But a permeable membrane, my love flowing into you
Passing back and forth
Exchanging love for love,
Lost in a world of our own

Always waiting

Alone in my heart, two directions to go
A pair of choices
One amber
One vermillion
Loss is inevitable, and the loss of love incomparable

To feel the grass beneath my feet
Cool and wet from morning dew
The last moments before the sun burns through
To walk those steps is my joy
To feel the dew, my pleasure.
Even after it is gone, it will still be in my heart
Always waiting
Always waiting

The Still Heat of the Morning

The chatter of cicadas
Rose above the whirring din of the window fan
I looked at you, your eyes smoldering in my heart
And we laid close, touching,
Breaths exchanged
Like one giant bellows

The life in you and me exchanged,
Passed back and forth in waves
In the still heat of the morning.

The Unasked Question

I want to know
I don't want to know
The question unasked swims in my head
And slaps my consciousness like
A whale's tail on the ocean

I love you dearly but am afraid
I cannot stay with you
If the answer
Is as I imagine

Like mighty King Hamlet, who was laid low
    With poison through his ear,
My heart could be broken by knowledge,
    My heart might wither and die

So I sit on a fulcrum

Do I ask the question?
    The answer could finish me
Or do I wait in unsettled love,
you pressed in my soul,
during nights of pleasure,
always wondering?

Flower on Still Water at Dawn

It starts simply
A kiss on your neck as my hand descends to your waist
And roams freely from there
Your body a playground for my fingertips

The silk robe you wore this morning at breakfast
Left in the hallway, discarded soon after I cupped your breasts and smelled the dried sweat from last night's dalliance
My mouth finds your body, your hips, your open thighs sweet like summer plums
You arch your back and say my name,
Finding the ecstasy I longed to give you

I kiss you deeply,
My beard thick with your wetness and scent
Bodies intertwined
Mine probing for entry
Our hands together, fingers interlaced
You inhale as you take me,
And I caress your soft lemniscate curves

The tick-tock of time we make our own,
A sacred dance whose steps we create
Like the Nataraj,
The universe consumed by the heat of our passion
Until all that remains is our unity of pleasure
Voiced in a primal speech known only for moments
Tongues dart and taste as heartbeats slow

You collapse into me

Breathless and quiet, eyes meet eyes
Smiles and kisses and laughter,
Whispered secrets of past and future,
Plans and promises and hopes and sighs

I lie with you, feeling your chest expand and contract
Your head in my arm
I stroke your hair

And kiss your head
And trace the curves of your back
I want to unfold the lotus petals I see blooming in you
Like the flower on still water at dawn

I think you are asleep
I don't want to wake you

Ribbons of Sunlight

Light streamed in through the window
    Cut in strips by the Venetian blind

She laid on the bed, stretched out gracefully,
    Having more the appearance of a sheet
    Thrown to the wind, landed softly against the mattress,
    Than of anything that ended up like that
    Through volition.
I traced the light beams with my fingers and stared in her eyes
    Fountains of beauty that steamed with spent passions,
Hearts still racing
Our bodies as one
With light spilled on her body,
    Lines made into curves,
    Ribbons of light made alive from her topography

I thought of that this morning
    When dawn's first light broke
I watched the sunrise in my rearview mirror,
    Wishing you could see it with me,
    Wishing I could be with you and trace the ribbons of sunlight
    That wash across your body

Mustard Leaves

A number of years back I planted mustard,
appropriate eating for the land I was in.
In my small plot four plants grew tall in the summer sun.
Broad leaves gave way to yellow flowers but got
eaten by parasites before I could cook most of them.

That same year my tomatoes were stolen by thirsty squirrels
and the ground cracked from lack of rain.

Between whiteflies on the leaves,
nematodes in the soil and worms in the fruit,
the harvest was poor that year.

Sweat stung my eyes and cut trails
through the dust on my forehead as
I worked to nurture my garden.

I thought about this as the fall chill set in and I sat
at the kitchen table,
winnowing the mustard seeds,
helping them through the holes of a sieve
as they left behind strands of dried flowers.

Lost Time

The power was out for a couple hours last week.
When it came back on the clock on the table across the room
flashed 12:00 for hours before
I started to set it
and then stopped.

My wife comes into my office
and comments on this often.

"What use is a clock," I say,
"when I have the window and my stomach and
the birds outside to let me know the time?"

She shakes her head and walks away,
her footsteps rhythmic as they fade down the hall into other rooms.

Tea Leaves Twice Used

I remember my mother's sewing kit from when I was young –
a collection of spools and pins,
needles stuck in a cushion shaped like a tomato,
cotton tape measure and chalk and shears
all stuffed in a macramé purse and hung on the inside of a closet door.

I don't know why I thought of this just now,
as I sip my tea from twice-used leaves.
Less flavor but still just as good
as the first time I poured.

The Apples I picked For Your This Morning

The apples I picked for you this morning -
    shiny, dwarfed,
       yellow and red
I don't know their flavor,
whether sweet or tart,
but I know their age,
as many had fallen
and were half-eaten on the ground,
picked over by deer and possums
       and other beasts.
They are as good now
as they will ever be.

Forgive the bruising -
    They bounced in my coat pockets
    as I rushed home to give them to you.

The spring rain falls gently under this tree

The spring rain falls gently under this tree,
        making bubbles in the puddles near where I stand.
As a lad I learned not to stand under a tree during a storm.
I can't remember why now. It is as good a shelter as any today.

The blue heron has returned to our pond,
a brief hiatus while en route to a more northern locale.
My footsteps must have been muffled by the rain.
Usually I can't get this close.

Just a few days from now, if history is good for prediction,
        the heron will leave this spot and continue its journey.
Where he goes is a mystery, as is the date of his return.
It is a time I will wait for, checking each day as the morning chill
approaches.

I must get back now.
The smell of fresh bread and garlic is still in my nose
and I am sure the eggplant is done baking as well.
Maybe after supper there will be enough light
        and the rain will silence my footsteps
so I can stand here again in the cool dusk air.

I Smell Your Hair in the Morning

I smell your hair in the morning
and the sweat on your body
as you lie in my arms,
the erotic story of my life with you,
Little kisses on your scalp to wake you from slumber

Part of me wants to let you sleep
another part longs to feel you closer
and taste you fully

I watch you breathe as you lie on me
        Feel your chest expand with each intake
        And fall a moment later

Your eyes, clear and blue, hidden from me
        Tucked behind lids but still in my memory
        And my thoughts

500 Arhats

500 arhats all classed and arranged in ancient manner,
My nose tingling from the heavy scent of years of incense burned in this place.

In meditation I sit
And try to remember ancient lessons lost to my past self,
Those teachings I at one time may have known,
The wisdom lost to the ravages of time.

The statues in this temple, all eyes penetrating my consciousness,
Sit unjudging but in full knowledge of my nature,
Who I am
My faults
My weaknesses
My desires
My hopes
My failings
My strengths

And in spite of this they sit with steady eyes
And gaze on me to offer encouragement and reinforce the dedication
I should want to have

Rice Fields on Stepped Mountains

Our passion feels ancient,
Like the rice fields on stepped mountains
From when time was measured solely by days of monsoon,
    Times to sow seed in the fertile mud,
    The rise and set of sunlight's rays
    The space between fire and dawn,
    Punctuated by low singing from afar,
    An ancient tongue known only to few,
    Swept on nighttime breezes across the mountains
    The steps nourished in rich mud
    Dark, black sustenance with long green shoots above

Our passion grows there
    Among the rice and snakes and beetles
    And cool permeating rains
    The mud our haven in the sun-quenched earth
    The mud our refuge where the fires are cooled and stoked
    Where the primal voice inside me calls your spirit name
    Where I feel your longing in the cracked mud of dry summers
    Dust on our bodies from planting seeds,
    The small shoots growing and finding purchase after the rain
    Your eyes clear and determined, heart light like rice flowers

I had hoped that rice would grow forever

Ritual Kumite

This spring I heard the mournful cry of a dove
who had tried to make a home on my balcony
This happens annually and the constant battle of man versus bird
A ritual kumite
Erupts within the silence of my apartment community

The doves always win, as I one day come home
to eggs in a nest, apparently erected and inhabited in the few hours I was gone,
And soon the babies with tiny heads and few feathers
wait gape-mouthed and desperate
as the mother feeds the others,
each looking as if it might die as it waits its turn
for the regurgitated seeds and insects

The babies remind me
That although man feels he must make his place and claim his birthright
as the top of the chain of interdependence
the smartest of all beasts
He is no less subject to the whims of nature
And cannot even defeat a bird when pressed
into ritual kumite

Less Time

You treat me like my life should be on hold
Ready for you whenever the moment arises
    That you are ready for me
    Whenever that may be
Like an egg timer toppled,
    The sands stopped, neither end emptying into the other
    The time at standstill
    The time an illusion
But time has kept marching forward,
    Lock-step at its own pace
Your hungry arms never have to wait for my embrace
    Like a fool I wait for you
    For when you are ready to receive me
    And leave when you are done
And what I find I am left with at the end of our time together
    Is simply less time

Morgan

You look well, I said
I had hoped that exchanging each other's belongings
    would cure something, fix my heartbreak
But I doubt it will

Only time heals the wounds of love
And I cannot hasten to that end any more
    than I can peel back the petals of an unbloomed rose
To find the glorious prize within

Svea

The park bench where we sat the morning I bought you breakfast and took you to the lighthouse is gone

I remember your ocean blue eyes as we had egg sandwiches and
talked about the morning
and the things on your mind

Your heart unsure of me

You smiled through the sadness in your eyes and words
I could see your heart unfold,
beaded droplets on rose petals

A cacophony of bird sound reminds me of that day
the way I wanted to embrace you as we walked
and sat together
the way I kissed you as we parted
      a simple peck
      a seed planted to grow a passion

A small taste at the buffet of your affections when I wanted the whole meal

Bonfire

Your hair smells of the bonfire from earlier
I can tell you are asleep from how your breathing changed a moment ago,
Gone from normal to shallow
as you lay on my chest,
Your skin on mine, your embrace a refuge
When I cannot see your eyes
Your touch like silk as your breath regains its waking state
I roll with you as you find your spot for nighttime slumber,
my arm around your waist
The bonfire is still strong in your hair, as it is in my heart
I don't want to fall asleep but I drift off.
I am most calm when holding you.

Urhu

It would be easy for me to call you selfish and believe my own words
But truthfully, you told me you were selfish early on,
That you wanted no more in return
Than you could be expected to give
And I expected too much, it seems,
And probably gave too much
But you were always there to urge me on
Playing me like a broken fiddle
Whose only song
Is the sad notes of the urhu, one string played over in whiny sing-song
Like a bird out of tune, singing my heart's lamentations

Absence

The other day you came into my mind
After your 30-year absence
I could still smell the sweat on your neck
And taste the tears that had dried on your lips

So tender
So new again

A Bridge

I shower when I come home from seeing you
Because your perfume on my skin
and the scent in my nose
Are not what I want to fall asleep to
And certainly not what I want to wake up with

I don't mean it as an insult
It's just that you are no more than a bridge
Between my old self and the new one
With shedded skin
That I will not feel the need to shower like I do tonight

Lotus

I listen to the stillness
That arises from within myself
From that place whence curiosity blooms
Where whispers generate themselves and turn into ideas
And the heart's flower blooms at unlikely times
Rising like a lotus from the murk of a pond's depths
Where nothing seems like it can grow again
But actually holds manifold nutrients
Hidden in the mud and silt
Of a broken heart

Pleasant Harbor

Your touch is electric
And when I kiss you our passions ignite
But I can't hold on forever
Hoping your heart changes course.
When someday you reach out to me to warm the sheets of your bed
And bring you pleasure in the night
I may no longer be there.
My heart, moored today in your pleasant harbor,
Might tomorrow find anchor points in other waters.
Until the wind carries me onward, I will be here,
Both excited and sad at our meetings,
Longing for your soft touch in my heart with your own.

Sleeping

Sleeping is harder without you by my side
But being without you has reminded me
Of all the ways I justified being with you
Despite your lack of commitment
And has helped me forget
All the ways I used to find to convince myself
that this was what I deserved

If I said I didn't miss you and your skin on mine and your kisses and
the sweat
while entwined in each other as a self-made caduceus,
I would be lying

And while my sleep has suffered a bit,
I will take it over the alternative

It is has been less sleep but better
Because of your absence

I Laid my Heart Bare for You

I laid my heart bare for you
As on an altar of our love
Where we together we dined
on each other's supple flesh
together finding sustenance
in our entwined tendrils
that drew a lifeblood from the ground
through our hearts
and beyond us

I laid my heart bare for you
And you chose to wipe your feet on it

Triangle Sandwiches

Those sandwiches you get at gas stations
the ones in the plastic triangles
with suspect-looking meats
and pimento cheese that has seen fresher days—
Eating those sandwiches is like playing gastro roulette

I knew your love would be hard won and delicious if I could get it
But I had no idea it would be as sad and mournful
as eating one of those sandwiches

If I told you I missed you
It would be in the same way I miss
That sad, tired pimento cheese

Sure, it is delicious going down
The taste familiar, the texture easy on my palate
But honestly, I am done playing roulette with my affections
And trying to make a gourmet meal from a triangle sandwich

Poison

I know you are poison
But the taste is sweet and tart
Like fresh mangoes plucked
And devoured still green
Their flesh unripe but the taste
Like the sweat on your back
When we pull the covers up in winter
    those beads that run down
    the valley of your spine
    then cool you when we rise at the sound of the bird

It seems so nourishing in the moment
But over time it reveals itself for what it is

Tall Boots

I told you that I had not done a good job
of guarding my heart
and offered it to you, and for a while
you accepted it and took it as a refuge

Or so you said

When you choose to be vulnerable with someone
heartbreak is what you sign up for
It is just an occasional unfortunate consequence of a beautiful
endeavor unfulfilled
not all endeavors are fruitful
Heartbreak as a matter of consequence
of things just not working out
is fair game

But you chose to be unkind

Saying that you relish in the passion we enjoyed
shared breath
eye contact
emotional intensity
moments of unspoken ecstasy
as I lost myself in the beauty of your eyes

Your smile was a facade
eyes looking for the next victim
as your tall boots strutted across the floor
to snatch a heart here and there for your collection of broken things
that once brought pleasure

Haiku

Tiny drops of rain,
Illuminated by sun,
Fall, form pools on ground.

Beautiful bird-forms
Flutter in my consciousness,
Fly beyond my grasp.

Red-feathered flutter,
Brilliant against dawn's thick fog,
Wakes me, disappears.

West wind carries scents
Of falling, sun-heated leaves.
Cools body, warms heart.

Winter's ice pellets,
Carried by late evening gusts,
Make music on glass.

All things accomplished
Daruma's eyes both darkened
Sunset approaching

Incense extinguished,
Heavy sweetness in cold air,
Arhats all watching

My love has flown
Like the geese of autumn
Rain clouds fill my heart

I smell long ago
Your hair and sweat and love
Eyes closed, rosebud lips

About the Author

Carl Weaver is a life-long writer who has dabbled in many forms of the craft. He is a poet, writer, cook, meat afficionado, Freemason, photographer, mechanic, fixit guy, maker, brewer, vintner, and more. Weaver has had more jobs than Carter's got liver pills and makes his home in Alexandria, Virginia. He hopes to one day have another cat.

He is the author of *Next Life in the Afternoon: A Journey Through Thailand* and *A Good Day to Die: Haiku in Traditional Form*.

www.ingramcontent.com/pod-product-compliance
Lightning Source LLC
Chambersburg PA
CBHW060904050426
42453CB00010B/1567